Say It Right

A Practical, User-Friendly,
Totally Unintimidating Guide to
Speaking Good English

By DIANE KAISER

Illustrations by Jerry McLaughlin

STARRHILL PRESS
WASHINGTON, D.C.

Designed by Momentum Design Studio
Edited by Nöelle Beatty

Printed and bound in U.S.A. by Bang Printing

Any inquiries should be directed to Starrhill Press, P.O. Box 21038,
Washington, DC 20009-0538, telephone (202) 387-9805.

Library of Congress Cataloguing-in-Publication Data
Kaiser, Diane
    Say it right: a practical, user-friendly, totally unintimidating
guide to speaking good English/by Diane Kaiser; illustrations by
Jerry McLaughlin.
    p. cm.
    ISBN 0-913515-95-7
    1. English language—Spoken English—Handbooks, manuals,
etc. 2. English language—Usage—Handbooks, manuals, etc.
I. Title. PE1074.8.K35 1994
    428.3—dc20   94-11472
                                            CIP

ACKNOWLEDGMENTS

Thank you to Liz Hill and Marty Starr who started it all.

To Nöelle Blackmer Beatty for her fine and thoughtful editing.

To Carl M. Hagge for kindly reviewing the manuscript.

To all my friends for their support, especially my sister Sash.

And to every participant in the writing workshops at Arkwright,

a heartfelt thank you.

To Tom

"Let your speech be always with grace, seasoned with salt."

Colossians 4:6

Contents

CONTENTS (continued)

CHAPTER 1

A Totally Different Guide to Speaking Good English

Most of us could use a little help with our English. How many times have you started to say something and caught yourself mid-sentence wondering, "Do I say 'I' here or 'me,' 'who' or 'whom,' 'me' or 'myself,' 'feel bad' or 'feel badly'?" How many times have you wondered, "Did I pronounce that word correctly?" Sometimes our mistakes can cause a few problems.

Let's say you're having dinner with your boss and her husband. The subject of summer holidays comes up. You say, "My husband, my children, and **myself** are planning to visit Montreal next summer. It's also a good opportunity for my husband and **I** to see his college roommate, **who** we haven't seen in years."

Uh-oh. Your boss's husband reads a lot and knows his English. You think you see him wince. You know you're using the right fork. Maybe he had a bad experience in Montreal. Maybe the vinaigrette is too sour. Guess again. If you had said, "My husband, my children, and **I** are planning to visit Montreal next summer. It's also a good opportunity for my husband and **me** to see his college roommate, **whom** we haven't seen in years," your English would have worked for you—not against you.

So your English is a little rusty. You admit it, but it's been a long time since junior high and those complex, confusing sentence diagrams. You find you've forgotten a lot of what you barely understood anyway. So you want a friendly little book to tell you what's correct and what isn't without getting into participles and gerunds and adverbs acting as adjectives. You're practical. You're busy. You want to speak good English but don't want to invest a lot of time in learning how. The only thing a traditional grammar book would do for you now is act as a reliable sedative.

Say It Right takes a lighthearted, cheerful, down-to-earth, and compassionate approach to speaking good English. We try to provide a little comic relief, and we focus only on the most common mistakes.

We hope you let this little book be a part of your everyday life. Keep it in the bathroom, in the glove compartment, on the porch, on the kitchen counter—wherever you'll be sure to read it. Underline, highlight, scribble comments in the margins. Forget ninth grade and the fact that you hated grammar. Relax. Take it at your own pace. Have fun. It's English. It's your language. Put it to work for you.

"There's no good speech save in Paris."

FRANÇOIS VILLON
Le Grand Testament
Ballade des Femmes de Paris

CHAPTER 2

Big Blunders & a Minor Indiscretion

It's true that you can get away with some grammatical mistakes in colloquial, or spoken, English. For example, you knock on your friend's backdoor. She calls, "Who is it?" You call back, **"It's me!"**

It may sound strange to your ears, but if you're going by the grammar book, the correct response is, **"It is I!"**

Here's another example: your phone rings. The caller says, "May I speak to Madame X, please?" You respond: **"This is her."** If you know your grammar, you know that to answer your caller correctly, you should say, **"This is she."**

But there are lots of phrases that are not considered correct even in spoken English. For example, if you say, "**Jim and me** took the train to Philadelphia," you're in trouble. If you say, "**Me and my sister** love to talk on the phone," you're in trouble. If you say, "This might be something **for you and he** to talk about," you're in trouble. If you say, "I started this business **for my wife and I** to make money," more trouble.

When it comes to using **I** and **me**, **him** and **her**, **he** and **she**, and **they** and **them**, we decided to let you know quickly—and without pain—what is technically correct and what isn't. In other words, we want you to know when you are breaking the rules. Then it's up to you.

"What is the use of a book," thought Alice,
"without pictures or conversations?"

LEWIS CARROLL
Alice's Adventures in Wonderland

When to Use Me

Many people use **I** in a sentence because they think **I** sounds more formal and, therefore, correct. Which sentence sounds right to you: number 1 or number 2?

1. The safari gave Harold and I the chance to be truly adventurous.

2. The safari gave Harold and me the chance to be truly adventurous.

Number 2 is correct. Here's a way to get this right. Practice this exercise, and eventually you'll be able to do it in your head while you're speaking.

Take out the words **Harold and**. Now say the sentence.

The safari gave I the chance to be truly adventurous.
The safari gave me the chance to be truly adventurous.

Obviously, the answer is **me**.

Since this is one of the biggest blunders in spoken English, let's look at a few more examples.

1. *Come with Roger and **I** to the top of the Empire State Building.*
2. *Come with Roger and **me** to the top of the Empire State Building.*

Number 2 is the right answer. Take out the words **Roger and**. Now say the sentence.

*Come with **I** to the top of the Empire State Building.*
*Come with **me** to the top of the Empire State Building.*

What sounds right is right. **Me** is correct.

1. *Last night, Ralph told Meri and **I** about his summer job as a hot-dog vendor.*
2. *Last night, Ralph told Meri and **me** about his summer job as a hot-dog vendor.*

Take out the words **Meri and**. Say the sentence.

*Last night, Ralph told **I** about his summer job as a hot-dog vendor.*
*Last night, Ralph told **me** about his summer job as a hot-dog vendor.*

Me is the right answer.

1. *The plumber met with my roommate and **I** to talk about the kitchen sink.*
2. *The plumber met with my roommate and **me** to talk about the kitchen sink.*

Take out the words **my roommate and**. Say the sentence.

*The plumber met with **I** to talk about the kitchen sink.*
*The plumber met with **me** to talk about the kitchen sink.*

Are you getting the hang of this? **Me** is the answer.

A few more examples:

YES:
*The waitress gave Joe and **me** a big smile and said, "Hello."*

NO:
*The waitress gave Joe and **I** a big smile and said, "Hello."*

DO:	DON'T:
Loretta taught Richard and **me** how to whistle for a cab.	Loretta taught Richard and **I** how to whistle for a cab.
The waiter poured Tom and **me** each a glass of Dom Perignon.	The waiter poured Tom and **I** each a glass of Dom Perignon.
He left his girlfriend and **me** in the lurch last night.	He left his girlfriend and **I** in the lurch last night.
If it's just for Harvey and **me**, please don't go to a lot of trouble with the hors d'oeuvres.	If it's just for Harvey and **I**, please don't go to a lot of trouble with the hors d'oeuvres.
The tickets to the rock concert are for **him** and **me**.	The tickets to the rock concert are for **he** and **I**.
My sister took Betsy and **me** for a ride in her yellow convertible.	My sister took Betsy and **I** for a ride in her yellow convertible.

After Between, Always Use Me, Never I

An easy way to remember this is that the **e** sound in **between** is just like the **e** sound in **me**. And along with **me** come **her**, **him**, or **them**—never **she**, **he**, or **they**. Pay attention to this one. It's another big blunder in spoken English.

YES:
*Between you and **me**, I think this new senator has a lot of charisma.*

NO:
*Between you and **I**, I think this new senator has a lot of charisma.*

DO:	DON'T:
Just **between** you and **me**, Lydia spends a fortune on cold cream.	Just **between** you and **I**, Lydia spends a fortune on cold cream.
What he said in his latest love letter is **between him** and **me**.	What he said in his latest love letter is **between he** and **I**.
There's a lot of affection **between her** and her Aunt Annie.	There's a lot of affection **between she** and her Aunt Annie.
Between you and **me**, Enrico is quite the philanderer.	**Between** you and **I**, Enrico is quite the philanderer.
I think there's too much competition **between her** and **me**.	I think there's too much competition **between she** and **I**.

"Be skillful in speech, that you may be strong…
words are braver than all fighting."

AUTHOR UNKNOWN
The Teaching for Merikare

When to Use I

Most of us instinctively use **I** as all or part of the subject of a sentence. But some of us are making a big blunder when we use **me** instead.

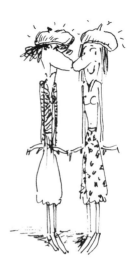

YES:
*Janine and **I** started the trend of wearing berets to class.*

NO:
*Janine and **me** started the trend of wearing berets to class.*

NO:
***Me** and Janine started the trend of wearing berets to class.*

DO:	DON'T:
Mary and **I** talked all night about opening a bookstore.	**Me** and Mary talked all night about opening a bookstore.
He and **I** played golf in the rain.	He and **me** played golf in the rain.
Quentin and **I** fell in love last week.	**Me** and Quentin fell in love last week.
Last spring, she and **I** went to Paris and discovered café au lait.	Last spring, she and **me** went to Paris and discovered café au lait.
Joe and **I** like to stay up late and watch old movies.	**Me** and Joe like to stay up late and watch old movies.

It's when we want to use **me** following **it is** and **it was** that spoken English and written English part ways. To be grammatically correct, you should use **I** after **it is** and **it was**.

It is I who worked the hardest on the float for the parade.

It was I, the proven underdog, who ended up winning the match.

It was I who called you around midnight and then hung up.

YES:
Who is the expert on Debussy?
It is I.
I am.
NO:
Who is the expert on Debussy?
It is me.

Usage is changing so much, however, that if you knock on your friend's door and call out, "**It's I!**" your friend might wonder why you sound so formal. "**It's me!**" is a minor indiscretion.

The best way to speak correctly and still sound like yourself is simply to change the sentence around.

I worked the hardest on the float for the parade.

Even though I was the underdog, I ended up winning the match.

I called you around midnight and then hung up.

"Who is the expert on Debussy? "I am."

And when you knock on your friend's door, you can always say, "It's Susan!"

With **she**, **he**, **we**, and **they**, the same rule applies as with **I**. After **is**, **was**, and **were**, use **she**, **he**, **we**, and **they**. Remember that you can always change these sentences so that they sound more natural to you.

YES:
*"May **I** speak to Professor Steinburger, please?"*
*"This is **he**." Or, "This is Professor Steinburger."*

NO:
*"May **I** speak to Professor Steinburger, please?"*
*"This is **him**."*

DO:

"May **I** speak to Estella, please?" "This is **she**." Or, "This is Estella."

It's **we** who told them about the applejack cider. Or, **We** told them about the applejack cider.

It's **he** who persuaded us to open a coffee shop on the corner. Or, **He** persuaded us to open a coffee shop on the corner.

It is **they** who started the ruckus. Or, **They** started the ruckus.

DON'T:

"May **I** speak to Estella, please?" "This is **her**."

It's **us** who told them about the applejack cider.

It's **him** who persuaded us to open a coffee shop on the corner.

It is **them** who started the ruckus.

DO:

DON'T:

It's **she** who started the rumor about bacteria in the drinking water. Or, **She** started the rumor about bacteria in the drinking water.

It's **her** who started the rumor about bacteria in the drinking water.

When...and When Not...to Use Myself

Very often, when we're uncertain whether to use **I** or **me**, we substitute **myself**. Sorry to say, this does not get rid of the problem. **Myself** isn't a replacement for **I** or **me**. Its uses are quite specific as you can see in the **Do** column below.

YES:
*Thank you for awarding Conway and **me** first prize in the dance contest.*

NO:
*Thank you for awarding Conway and **myself** first prize in the dance contest.*

THANKS

DO:	DON'T:
Jerry, Daphne, and **I** are undecided about when to open the restaurant.	Jerry, Daphne, and **myself** are undecided about when to open the restaurant.
Julio sang a love song to the duchess and **me** last night.	Julio sang a love song to the duchess and **myself** last night.
I will assign the project to Flannery or **you** next week.	I will assign the project to Flannery or **yourself** next week.
Officer Williams and **I** were on duty that night.	**Myself** and Officer Williams were on duty that night.
I always give **myself** plenty of time.	
I talk to **myself** a lot.	
I **myself** am not involved.	
I'm just not **myself** lately.	

If You Want to Know Why...

RULE: Pronouns used as or relating to the subject of the sentence are different from pronouns used as objects in a sentence.

Subject Pronouns: **I, She, He, We, They**

Object Pronouns: **Me, Her, Him, Us, Them**

What is a subject pronoun?

Subject pronouns relate to the subject of the sentence. The subject is the person, place, or thing the sentence is talking about. A subject can be simple or complete. It's complete when accompanied by words that describe it.

A subject pronoun in action: It is **I** who bought the yellow coupe.

It is the simple subject of the sentence above.
Is is the verb that links the subject to the subject pronoun **I.** In other words, **It = I.**

Here's another example: The happiest ones were **you** and **I.**

The happiest ones is the complete subject of the sentence above.
Were is the verb linking the complete subject to the subject pronouns **you** and **I.**
So **the happiest ones = you and I.**

One more: The worst skaters on the team are **Jack, Josie**, and **I.**

The worst skaters is the complete subject.
Are is the linking verb.
Jack, Josie, and **I** are the nouns and pronoun related to the subject.
So **Jack, Josie, and I = the worst skaters.**

RULE: Object pronouns are used as objects of a preposition, direct objects, and indirect objects.

Object Pronouns: **Me, Her, Him, Us, Them**

An object pronoun can be an object of a preposition. Prepositions are those little words like **of, by, for, to, up, on, with, between, from, over, under,** etc. Their objects follow them and together they make a prepositional phrase.

Object pronouns used as objects of a preposition:

Between you and **me**, I think Marlene should give up on voice lessons.

John asked me to come **with** Louise and **him** to the cocktail party.

Mother gave these heirlooms **to** Edward and **me** last year.

Please send these widgets **to** both the customer and **me** by Monday.

If the party is **for** Judy and **me**, please make sure there is cheesecake on the menu.

Object pronouns also act as direct or indirect objects in a sentence. This simply means they receive the action of the verb or they tell to or for whom, or to or for what, something is done.

Object pronouns used as sentence objects:

Harold **mentioned him** and **her** in his memoirs.

The foreman **ordered him** and his friend off the line.

The French professor **told** Alain and **me** to work on our accents.

The city **rewarded** both **us** and our neighbors for our recycling campaign.

She gave **him** a black leather jacket for Halloween.

Pop Quiz

1. Just between you and (I, me), George has put on a few pounds.

2. I'll fax the drawings to (he, him) and the client next week.

3. The supervisor told Mary and (I, me) to use our creativity.

4. It is (I, me) who decided to major in ornithology because of my interest in parrots.

5. I paid (she, her) and the consultant far too much for their advice.

6. It was (we, us) who led the walking tour through the Adirondacks.

7. Please don't come with Donald and (I, me) on our first date.

8. The issue is between (she and I) (her and me).

9. He spoke to Susan, James, and (I, myself, me) about his love of thatched cottages.

10. My sister and (I, me) used to love to make chocolate cakes with cherry icing.

ANSWERS: 1) me, 2) him, 3) me, 4) I, 5) her, 6) we, 7) me, 8) her and me, 9) me, 10) I

"Talking with a friend
is nothing else but thinking aloud."

ADDISON

CHAPTER 3

Cantankerous Couples

English is full of cranky, cantankerous word couples that really like being difficult. They get a kick out of the fact that we frequently misuse them and love to see us with egg on our faces.

Let's take their fun away. Choose your favorite couple and get to know them. Practice putting them in sentences. So what if you feel a little silly going around saying things like, "For the past week, I have **lain** awake every night," or, "My hair is adversely **affected** by all this humidity." Go ahead. It's good mental exercise, and after a little bit of this, the couple will never trouble you again.

> **Lay** and **Lie**
> **Good** and **Well**
> **Can** and **May**
> **Fewer** and **Less**
> **As** and **Like**
> **Feel Bad** and **Feel Badly**
> **Sit** and **Set**
> **Farther** and **Further**
> **Sensual** and **Sensuous**
> **Affect** and **Effect**
> **Then** and **Than**
> **Continuous** and **Continual**
> **Uninterested** and **Disinterested**
> **Regardless** and **Irregardless**
> **Imply** and **Infer**

Lay and Lie

Lay means <u>to put</u> or <u>to place</u>. Its three parts are **lay, laid, laid**.
Like this:

"**Lay** the blanket over here," she said, "next to this handsome lifeguard."
(The action is taking place right now—in the present.)

Yesterday, we **laid** the blanket near a different handsome lifeguard.
(The action took place in the past—yesterday.)

Since summer started, we have **laid** the blanket near several different lifeguards.
(The action started a while ago, in the past, but continues into the present.)

Lie means <u>to recline</u>. Its three parts are **lie, lay, lain**.
Like this:

"Why don't you **lie** down?" she said. "Your eyes look dark and haunted." *(She is speaking right now—in the present.)*

Last night, I **lay** awake for hours concerned with what she said. *(I **lay** awake last night. Last night is past. It's over.)*

I have **lain** awake for a week now, and I'm still worrying. *(This sleeplessness started a week ago, but it still continues.)*

These are such tricky words that you may simply have to memorize the meaning and three parts of each. Sometimes making up a funny little ditty or poem helps:

"Lay, laid, laid," sang the innocent maid.
"Lie, lay, lain," sang her wily swain.

YES:
*I **lay** awake for hours last night worrying about my new hair color.*
NO:
*I **laid** awake for hours last night worrying about my new hair color.*

DO:

"Please **lay** the newspaper down for one minute," she pleaded.

I **laid** the blanket over there yesterday, near the hot-dog stand.

I have **lain** awake every night since the rains began.

"Why don't you **lie** across my big brass bed?" the folksinger crooned.

"**Lie** down and go to sleep," her mother said wearily.

I decided to **lie** down and take a long nap.

DON'T:

"Please **lie** the newspaper down for one minute," she pleaded.

I **lay** the blanket over there yesterday, near the hot-dog stand.

I have **laid** awake every night since the rains began.

"Why don't you **lay** across my big brass bed?" the folksinger crooned.

"**Lay** down and go to sleep," her mother said wearily.

I decided to **lay** down and take a long nap.

Good and Well

Good describes a person, place, thing, or idea.
Well describes an action word or refers to health.

YES:
*He speaks Swahili **well**.*
NO:
*He speaks Swahili **good**.*

DO:

You look **good** today.
(This means your appearance is pleasing. You might be wearing a flattering color or perhaps you've just had your hair cut or you've finally shaved.)

You look **well** today.
(This means you look healthy, fit, and well rested with no circles under your eyes.)

Harry has such a **good** disposition.

DON'T:

"How are you?" "I'm **well**, thank you."

"How are you?" "I'm **good**, thank you."

Maude sings arias so **well**.

Maude sings arias so **good**.

His old pickup truck still runs **well**.

His old pickup truck still runs **good**.

Did you sleep **well**?

Did you sleep **good**?

Can and May

Can means you have the ability to do something.
May asks permission or suggests possibility.

YES:
*He **may** assign you the job of feeding the tigers.*
*He knows you **can** do it.*

DO:	DON'T:
May I invite you to dinner?	**Can** I invite you to dinner?
May I speak to you in private, please?	**Can** I speak to you in private, please?
You **may** have my phone number.	You **can** have my phone number.
You **may** borrow my snowblower.	You **can** borrow my snowblower.
Can you finish your novel next week?	
Can you pick up these books so that I **can** dust my desk?	
Don't you think you **can** learn French while commuting to work?	
Can he resist the temptation to eat the rest of the chocolate truffles?	

Fewer and Less

If you can count the objects or people you're describing, use **fewer**. If you can't, use **less**. Most of the time, we use **less** correctly. It's **fewer** we tend to botch.

YES:
*I weigh **fewer** pounds than Lottie.*
NO:
*I weigh **less** pounds than Lottie.*

DO:	DON'T:
There are **fewer** grams of fat in this salad dressing than in that one made with mayonnaise.	There are **less** grams of fat in this salad dressing than in that one made with mayonnaise.
John decided to eat **fewer** eggs for breakfast.	John decided to eat **less** eggs for breakfast.
We saw **fewer** cars on the road today because of the holiday.	We saw **less** cars on the road today because of the holiday.
I walk **fewer** miles each morning than Christine.	I walk **less** miles each morning than Christine.
There is **less** traffic on the parkway today than usual.	
She earns **less** as an acrobat than he does as a magician.	

As and Like

Use **as** or **as if** if the words following them make a sentence (there is a subject and an action word or verb). **Like** was never meant to be used every time we take a breath: "I mean it's **like** crazy, the way we **like** overuse **like**."

YES:
*The picnic went just **as** we planned. (Note that after **as**, there is a sentence with the subject, **we**, and the action word, **planned**. We planned.)*

NO:
*The picnic went just **like** we planned.*

DO:	DON'T:
Theodore felt **as if** their visit would never end.	Theodore felt **like** their visit would never end.
James always acted **as if** he knew what he was doing.	James always acted **like** he knew what he was doing.
It looked **as if** we might not make it to Tahiti.	It looked **like** we might not make it to Tahiti.
John brought home six pounds of broccoli, just **as** he said he would.	John brought home six pounds of broccoli, just **like** he said he would.
Just **as** she said, the coffee was terrible.	Just **like** she said, the coffee was terrible.
Her hair looked **like** a hawthorne bush in a hurricane.	
	"Well," I said to her, "**like** what do you mean?"
	Like how can you say that?
	Do you think I'm **like** totally obtuse?

Feel Bad and Feel Badly

If you feel guilty or disappointed or otherwise distressed, you **feel bad** about something. You **feel badly** when your fingers or toes are numb or asleep or missing. In other words, you are unable to **feel** in a normal manner.

YES:
*His toes **felt badly** after he wore his new wing tips.*

NO:
*His toes **felt bad** after he wore his new wing tips.*

DO:	DON'T:
I **felt bad** about spilling tomato juice on her white sofa.	I **felt badly** about spilling tomato juice on her white sofa.
Don't you **feel bad** about cutting her hair so short?	Don't you **feel badly** about cutting her hair so short?
I **felt bad** about backing into his car.	I **felt badly** about backing into his car.
We **feel bad** about interrupting your dinner party.	We **feel badly** about interrupting your dinner party.
Louise **felt bad** about missing her clarinet lesson.	Louise **felt badly** about missing her clarinet lesson.
Her fingers were **feeling badly** because her gloves were full of holes.	Her fingers were **feeling bad** because her gloves were full of holes.
I **feel** so **bad** about not getting in touch with you.	I **feel** so **badly** about not getting in touch with you.

Sit and Set

If your legs ache, and you're tired of standing, you **sit.**

If you're placing something somewhere, you **set** it on a table, a chair, your head, or the dashboard of your car.

YES:
Set the rocker by the fire.
NO:
Sit the rocker by the fire.

DO:	DON'T:
Sit in the rocker by the fire.	**Set** in the rocker by the fire.
Please, **sit** down.	Please, **set** down.
I decided to **sit** down in the plush, yellow armchair.	I decided to **set** down in the plush, yellow armchair.
Sit yourself down and rest a spell.	**Set** yourself down and rest a spell.
"**Set** the armoire in that corner," she said to the big, burly man.	"**Sit** the armoire in that corner," she said to the big, burly man.
The waiter always **sets** the flowers in the center of each table.	The waiter always **sits** the flowers in the center of each table.

Farther and Further

Farther applies to additional distance.

Further applies to extra amounts or extra time or just plain extra.

YES:
*Have you ever seen the **farther** side of the moon?*

NO:
*Have you ever seen the **further** side of the moon?*

DO:	DON'T:
As we went **farther** into the jungle, the light dimmed.	As we went **further** into the jungle, the light dimmed.
Home was **farther** away than we thought.	Home was **further** away than we thought.
He refuses to discuss this any **further**.	He refuses to discuss this any **farther**.
She had a **further** reason for defying the court.	She had a **farther** reason for defying the court.
My legs won't carry me any **farther**.	My legs won't carry me any **further**.
Los Angeles is **farther** away than Santa Barbara.	Los Angeles is **farther** away than Santa Barbara.

Sensual and Sensuous

Sensual has to do with that old demon, sex.
Sensuous has to do with the senses.

*After she left the room, her perfume
lingering **sensuously**, he found himself
thinking **sensual** thoughts.*

You can make your own **Do** and **Don't**
lists on this one, but we'll get you started:

DO:	DON'T:
A cup of hot tea on a January afternoon is a **sensuous** delight.	A cup of hot tea on a January afternoon is a **sensual** delight.
She listens to the sound of the wind, smells the first scent of autumn; she is **sensuously** awake.	She listens to the sound of the wind, smells the first scent of autumn; she is **sensually** awake.
Eunice had never thought of George as a **sensual** being—until last night.	Eunice had never thought of George as a **sensuous** being—until last night.

Affect and Effect

Affect means <u>to influence</u>.

> *His bunion was always **affected** by the weather.*
>
> *I was **affected** by the gentle tone of his voice.*
>
> *The company's profits were **affected** byEuropean competition.*

Effect means <u>to bring about</u> or <u>to accomplish something</u>.

> *I am trying to **effect** a change in my weight by giving up hot fudge sundaes.*
>
> *He **effected** attitudes in the department by giving everyone raises.*

Effect also means <u>result</u>.

> *His persuasive charm seemed to have no **effect** on her at all.*

> YES: *Her hair was **affected** by the high humidity.*
> NO: *Her hair was **effected** by the high humidity.*

DO:	DON"T:
Gandhi's philosophy **effected** great change.	Gandhi's philosophy **affected** great change.
The **effect** of all this caffeine is that I'm taking a midnight stroll.	The **affect** of all this caffeine is that I'm taking a midnight stroll.
He said himself that her perfume adversely **affected** his sinuses.	He said himself that her perfume adversely **effected** his sinuses.
His poetry has **affected** all of us in some way.	His poetry has **effected** all of us in some way.

Then and Than

Then has to do with <u>time</u>.

> ***Then*** *he decided to cash in his chips and go home.*

> *He knew **then** what to do.*

> ***Then*** *it was inevitable that he tell his wife he had lost the entire contents of the checking account.*

Use **than** when you're making <u>comparisons</u>.

> *Mrs. Swinson is a better poker player **than** Mrs. Taylor.*

> *Since her expression never gives her away, she wins more games **than** her friend.*

YES:
*Nothing is better **than** French onion soup on a cold winter night.*

NO:
*Nothing is better **then** French onion soup on a cold winter night.*

DO:	DON'T:
After we visit the museum, **then** we'll stop at a cafe.	After we visit the museum, **than** we'll stop at a cafe.
When we hear his side of the story, **then** we'll know what to do.	When we hear his side of the story, **than** we'll know what to do.
Richard wears better looking suits **than** Marshall does.	Richard wears better looking suits **then** Marshall does.

DO:

DON'T:

DO:	DON'T:
She knew **then** that he loved Bernice more **than** her.	She knew **than** that he loved Bernice more **then** her.
She has a rounder face **than** her sister.	She has a rounder face **then** her sister.

"Speech is a mirror of the soul: as a man speaks, so is he."

PUBLILIUS SYRUS
Maxim 1073

Continuous and Continual

Continuous means <u>without stopping</u>, in other words, with no interruptions.

*We had two days and nights of **continuous** rain.*

*The television was on **continuously,** hour after hour.*

Continual means that something is <u>constantly recurring</u>, happening again and again, but <u>with interruptions</u>.

*People were **continually** interrupting each other at the meeting.*

*He's a fine actor because he **continually** practices his craft.*

YES:
*The ringing in her left ear was **continuous.***
NO:
*The ringing in her left ear was **continual.***

DO:	DON'T:
He ran **continuously** for ten miles.	He ran **continually** for ten miles.
He **continually** tries to teach her good manners.	He **continuously** tries to teach her good manners.
The lightning flashed and the thunder rumbled **continuously** through the night.	The lightning flashed and the thunder rumbled **continually** through the night.

DO:

Bernie has worked **continuously** for the past year on his thesis.

John's cat, Mrs. Danvers, **continually** raked her claws through his new carpet.

DON'T:

Bernie has worked **continually** for the past year on his thesis.

John's cat, Mrs. Danvers, **continuously** raked her claws through his new carpet.

"Talking and eloquence are not the same: to speak, and to speak well, are two things. A fool may talk, but a wise man speaks."

BEN JONSON
Timber; or, Discoveries Made upon Men and Matter

Uninterested and Disinterested

When you're **uninterested** in something or someone, you really don't care about it or them. You're simply not interested.

*Michael is **uninterested** in the workings of the internal combustion engine.*

*I am **uninterested** in the fellow who leers at me in the company cafeteria.*

When you're **disinterested**, you're neutral, you're impartial, you're fair, you're without prejudice.

*Everyone believes a judge should be **disinterested**.*

*The movie critic was known for his experience and **disinterest**.*

YES:
*I'm completely **uninterested** in learning how to play bridge.*

NO:
*I'm completely **disinterested** in learning how to play bridge.*

DO:	DON'T:
She was **uninterested** in the political process.	She was **disinterested** in the political process.
John was **uninterested** in taking a trip to Nepal.	John was **disinterested** in taking a trip to Nepal.

DO:

DON'T:

The umpire was known for his **disinterest** and fair play.

The umpire was known for his **uninterest** and fair play.

"I'm totally **uninterested** in going out to dinner with you," she said.

"I'm totally **disinterested** in going out to dinner with you," she said.

"Please show a bit of **disinterest** and give me a chance," he pleaded.

"Please show a bit of **uninterest** and give me a chance," he pleaded.

Regardless and Irregardless

Nothing could be simpler—just don't use **irregardless**. Take the word and throw it over the back fence.

Why? Irregardless takes **regardless** (a perfectly good, solid word) and tries to make it sound more important by adding the useless prefix: *ir.* (The prefix is useless because you already have the negative suffix: *less.*)

YES:
Regardless *of his typing skills, he insists on typing his memoirs himself.*

NO:
Irregardless *of his typing skills, he insists on typing his memoirs himself.*

DO:	DON'T:
Regardless of the consequences, she ate the whole box of chocolates.	**Irregardless** of the consequences, she ate the whole box of chocolates.
Regardless of her myopia, she took the driving test without her glasses.	**Irregardless** of her myopia, she took the driving test without her glasses.
Regardless of her fear of the water, she closed her eyes and jumped into the pool.	**Irregardless** of her fear of the water, she closed her eyes and jumped into the pool.
Regardless of his rumpled appearance, he decided to go to the interview.	**Irregardless** of his rumpled appearance, he decided to go to the interview.
Regardless of his shyness, he smiled at her anyway.	**Irregardless** of his shyness, he smiled at her anyway.

Imply and Infer

When you **imply** something, you <u>insinuate or suggest</u>.

> *She **implied** that she wasn't interested in the construction job.*

> *In his speech, Renaldo **implied** that he would support the recycling effort.*

When you **infer** something, you <u>come to a conclusion</u> after you've analyzed the facts or whatever evidence you've got.

> *After studying the sky, Miles **inferred** that the picnic would be cancelled.*

> *When she saw the man dressed in a dinner jacket at noon, she **inferred** that he was a waiter.*

YES:
*He studied the painting with such intensity, she **inferred** he must be an art critic.*

NO:
*He studied the painting with such intensity, she **implied** he must be an art critic.*

DO:

Maria's arched eyebrows **implied** her disapproval.

She **implied** that she thought him very attractive.

DON'T:

Maria's arched eyebrows **inferred** her disapproval.

She **inferred** that she thought him very attractive.

DO:	DON'T:
The instructor **implied** that I had done very well on the exam.	The instructor **inferred** that I had done very well on the exam.
The bartender **inferred** from the man's slurred speech that he had had his share of gin.	The bartender **implied** from the man's slurred speech that he had had his share of gin.
She **inferred** from his accent that he must be from the south of Wales.	She **implied** from his accent that he must be from the south of Wales.

Pop Quiz

1. She (lay, laid) awake for hours plotting revenge.

2. Bergen decided to eat (fewer, less) eggs for breakfast.

3. (Can, May) I walk you to your door?

4. Marshmallows taste good (like, as) marshmallows should.

5. Enrico (felt bad, felt badly) about leaving her stranded in a snowdrift.

6. I was (affected, effected) by his quick smile and the way he looked in blue jeans.

7. Why don't you (sit, set) over by the window and catch the sea breeze?

8. Honeoye Falls is (further, farther) away than Chautauqua Falls.

9. The sky looked (as if, like) it might release a deluge any minute.

10. He decided to (lie, lay) down on the queen's bed.

11. His body language (implied, inferred) that he didn't want the job.

12. He told her he loved her more (then, than) he loved his Harley.

13. The lava flowed (continuously, continually) from the island's only volcano.

14. Martha was completely (disinterested, uninterested) in the correct use of the semicolon.

Can you find the mistakes in this scenario?

Lorenzo and His Attentions

I felt so badly after I told Lorenzo I was completely disinterested in him and his dinner invitation that I called him back and said, "Irregardless of how I feel about your attentions and strange habit of wearing mismatched socks, I will go out with you. But can I ask one favor? Please wear a pair of socks that match."

Lorenzo replied that his emotions had been radically effected by the sensual perfume I wear; so much so that he had laid awake for three nights dreaming of me wearing a yellow dress and laying on a chaise lounge, continuously eating marzipan and reading a novel. He said all he wanted to do was set by me in a restaurant and inhale my perfume. He also said he would like search through his sock drawer for a matching pair, but if it came down to it, he would take things one step farther and like buy a new pair.

I was quite touched by this and decided that maybe I wasn't so disinterested in Lorenzo and his attentions after all.

Answers: I **felt** so **bad** after I told Lorenzo I was completely **uninterested** in him and his dinner invitation that I called him back and said, "**Regardless** of how I feel about your attentions and strange habit of wearing mismatched socks, I will go out with you. But **may** I ask one favor? Please wear a pair of socks that match."

Lorenzo replied that his emotions had been radically **affected** by the **sensuous** perfume I wear; so much so that he had **lain** awake for three nights dreaming of me wearing a yellow dress and **lying** on a chaise lounge, **continually** eating marzipan and reading a novel. He said all he wanted to do was **sit** by me in a restaurant and inhale my perfume. He also said he would search through his sock drawer for a matching pair, but if it came down to it, he would take things **one** step **further** and buy a new pair.

I was quite touched by this and decided that maybe I wasn't so **uninterested** in Lorenzo and his attentions after all.

"With thee conversing I forget all time,
All seasons, and their change; all please alike."

MILTON
Paradise Lost

CHAPTER 4

The Old Who/Whom Dilemma:

A Practical Solution You Didn't Learn in High School

Maybe you gave up on **who** and **whom** a long time ago. It's understandable, given the mental gymnastics we went through in grammar class to use those words correctly. Many of us decided it wasn't worth the trouble, gave up on **whom** entirely, and stuck with **who**. Let's bring **whom** back with this simple exercise, an approach that takes a route around grammar.

STEP 1. Look at the sentence with the **who/whom** dilemma.

Who/Whom went for coffee this morning?

STEP 2. If the sentence asks a question, try to answer it using **him**. If you can, then **whom** is the answer. If you can't, then **who** is the word you want. A little memory device: both **him** and **whom** end in **m**.

Answer: **He** went for coffee this morning.

Answer: **Him** went for coffee this morning.

STEP 3. **He** obviously is the right word, so **who** is the answer.

STEP 4. **Who** went for coffee this morning?

Here's another one:

STEP 1. For **who/whom** are you working now?

STEP 2. *Answer:*

I'm working for **him**.

I'm working for **he**.

STEP 3. Obviously **him** works, so **whom** is correct.

STEP 4. For **whom** are you working now?

And another:

STEP 1. **Who/Whom** did you call last night?

STEP 2. *Answer:*

I called **him**.

I called **he**.

STEP 3. **Him** again. **Whom** is the answer.

STEP 4. **Whom** did you call last night?

Are you getting the hang of this? Why don't you try a few on your own?

1. **Who/Whom** do you like best?
2. With **who/whom** did you go to the roller rink?
3. **Who/Whom** won the award for best director?
4. To **who/whom** did you send the chain letter?
5. **Who/Whom** do you think is the most charming?

Answers: 1) whom, 2) whom, 3) who, 4) whom, 5) who

What if the sentence with the **who/whom** dilemma doesn't ask a question?

*Susan McDee, **who/whom** in my opinion you overlooked, is an excellent candidate.*

STEP 1. Look at the part of the sentence between the commas.

*...**who/whom** in my opinion you overlooked...*

STEP 2. Turn that part of the sentence into a question.
***Who/Whom** did you overlook?*

STEP 3. Answer the question using **he** or **him**.
*(Even though Susan McDee is obviously not a **he** or a **him**, this little trick still works.)*

> I overlooked **he**.
> I overlooked **him**.

STEP 4. **Him** works, so **whom** is the answer.

STEP 5. Susan McDee, **whom** in my opinion you overlooked, is an excellent candidate.

Here's another one:

> *Valentino, **who/whom** we think is most talented, should win the archery contest.*

STEP 1. Look at the words between the commas.
*...**who/whom** we think is most talented...*

STEP 2. Turn that part of the sentence into a question.
***Who/Whom** do we think is most talented?*

STEP 3. Answer the question using **he** or **him**.
*We think **he** is most talented.*
*We think **him** is most talented.*

STEP 4. **He** works, so **who** is the word you want.

STEP 5. Valentino, **who** we think is most talented, should win the archery contest.

Ready to try a few?

A. Brook, **who/whom** we believe has the greenest thumb, should run the gardening club.

STEP 1. Write down the part of the sentence between the commas.
STEP 2. Make this part of the sentence a question.
STEP 3. Answer the question using **he** or **him**.
Step 4. Write your final sentence using **who** or **whom**.

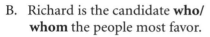

B. Richard is the candidate **who/whom** the people most favor.

STEP 1. Starting with **who/whom**, turn the sentence into a question.
STEP 2. Answer the question using **he** or **him**.
STEP 3. Which one works?
STEP 4. What's your final answer?

C. **Who/Whom** are we going to visit in Lima?

STEP 1. Answer the question using **he** or **him**.
STEP 2. Which one works? **He** or **him**?
STEP 3. Write the sentence using **who** or **whom**.

D. George is a man **who/whom** everyone respects.

STEP 1. Starting with **who/whom**, turn the sentence into a question.
STEP 2. Answer the question using **he** or **him**.
STEP 3. **He** or **him**? **Who** or **whom**? Write the final sentence.

E. Thomas is a man **who/whom** listens well.

    STEP 1. Turn the sentence into a question.
    STEP 2. Answer using **he** or **him**.
    STEP 3. Write the final sentence.

Answers: A) who, B) whom, C) whom, D) whom, E) who

Now you're completely on your own.

1. Rita, **who/whom** we feel is best qualified, should get the job of talk-show host.
2. To **who/whom** have you decided to bequeath your Nash Rambler?
3. **Who/Whom** did you forget to call?
4. He was an ardent orator **who/whom** Juliette truly admired.
5. With **who/whom** are you attending the inauguration?

Answers: 1) who, 2) whom, 3) whom, 4) whom, 5) whom

*He was an ardent orator **who/whom**
Juliette truly admired.*

"Monkeys, who very sensibly refrain from speech,
lest they should be set to earn their livings . . ."

KENNETH GRAHAME
The Golden Age

CHAPTER 5

Red Lights & Alarm Bells

After reading this chapter, you will have sentenced yourself to a lifetime of red lights and alarm bells. When you know the grammatically correct way to use the words in this chaper, you'll be amazed at how often you'll hear them used incorrectly. Lights will flash and alarms will jangle every time you hear these words misused. If you don't want to read this chapter, we understand.

"Don't talk
unless you can improve the silence."

PROVERB

The Trouble with Hopefully

Hopefully means <u>with hope</u>, not <u>I hope that</u>.

It appears that so few people are aware of the meaning that you can, no doubt, join the ranks and get away with misusing **hopefully.** But if you find yourself in the company of someone you vaguely suspect speaks good English, watch your step.

YES:
*Rover waited **hopefully** for his bone.*

NO:
***Hopefully**, Alexander will give Rover his bone.*

DO:

I hope that you will wear socks.

We hope this year brings prosperity.

I hope I'm learning to control my outbreaks of paranoia.

We hope we'll see the falling star.

John waited **hopefully** for his blind date.

I watched him **hopefully** as he skated toward the goal.

DON'T:

Hopefully, you will wear socks.

Hopefully, this year will bring prosperity.

Hopefully, I'm learning to control my outbreaks of paranoia.

Hopefully, we'll see the falling star.

Watch Out for Everyone and Everybody

Believe it or not, **everybody** and **everyone** really represent <u>one person</u>, not several. So do the other words ending in "body" or "one," such as **anybody** and **no one**. Since they stand for only one person, the correct words to use with them are **his** and **her, he** and **she,** and **himself** and **herself**.

YES:
*Everybody said **he** or **she** had eaten too many pancakes for breakfast.*

NO:
*Everybody at the breakfast table said **they** had eaten too many pancakes.*

DO:	DON'T:
Everyone in the group believes **he** or **she** is a movie star.	**Everyone** in the group believes **they** are a movie star.
Anybody can play the game if **he** or **she** is willing to practice long hours.	**Anybody** can play the game if **they** are willing to practice long hours.
Everybody took **himself** or **herself** very seriously at the audition.	**Everybody** took **themselves** very seriously at the audition.
Everybody enjoyed **herself** at the luncheon.	**Everybody** enjoyed **themselves** at the luncheon.

HINT: If all of these seem awkward to you, and you don't like this **his/her** business, your best bet is to get rid of **everybody** or **everyone** and just say the sentence another way.

They all said they had eaten too many pancakes for breakfast.

They all believe they are movie stars.

You can play the game if you're willing to practice long hours.

"One great use of words is to hide our thoughts."

VOLTAIRE

The Truth about Literally

Literally means <u>exactly as the words say</u>. So if someone tells you that she was **literally** tearing her hair out, ask her if she has any left.

Someone could **literally** be down to his last dime. Someone could **literally** back his car into your front bumper or **literally** shave his head. An elephant could **literally** step on your toes.

But don't use **literally** to mean <u>really</u> or <u>actually</u>. For example, he was **literally** going out of his mind.

DON'T:

He was **literally** beside himself with anger.

Susan was **literally** down in the dumps.

Marcel **literally** overwhelmed her with poems, roses, and chocolates.

She **literally** hit the roof.

He **literally** was climbing the walls. (*Unless, of course, he's painting his house or climbing Kilimanjaro.*)

She **literally** acts like another person when she's around her art teacher.

*Someone could **literally** shave his head.*

Can you find the mistakes in this scenario?

Harriet and the Proposal

You are sitting in an orange, molded-plastic chair and have just finished a cheeseburger deluxe without onions. Your handsome friend across the table is still working his way through a triple deluxe with a double order of fries. You wait.

He drains his shake, wads the napkin, looks at you dreamily, and says, "Harriet, you and me, we make quite a pair. Just between you and I, the way I see it, you and myself are meant to be. What I want to do, Harriet, is take you and I away from all this. So I talked to my buddy Jack, and him and me come up with a plan. He said, seeing that it's for you and myself, he'll lend us his '64 Olds. Hopefully, it still runs. What do you say?"

Answers: "Harriet, you and **I**, we make quite a pair. Just between you and **me**, the way I see it, you and **I** are meant to be. What I want to do, Harriet, is take you and **me** away from all this. So **I** talked to my buddy Jack, and **he** and **I came** up with a plan. He said, seeing that it's for you and **me**, he'll lend us his '64 Olds. **I hope** it still runs. What do you say?"

CHAPTER 6

Taking Out the Trash

Every now and then, it's a good idea to listen to the words you're using and clean house. You may be cluttering your communication with words and phrases that need to go in the nearest garbage can.

Keep:	Throw Out:
this	this here
these	these there
that	that there
those	them there
he, she, it doesn't	he, she, it don't
anyway	anyways
anywhere	anywheres
since	being as
himself	hisself
regardless	irregardless
nowhere	nowheres
somewhere	somewheres
should have, shouldn't have	should of, shouldn't of
may have, could have	may of, could of
going to, trying to	fixing to
he and I, we	him and me, we

Keep:	Throw Out:
she and he, they	her and him, they
try to	try and
themselves	theirselves
a way to go	a ways to go
anyway	nohow
am not, is not, are not, have not, has not	ain't
I, you, he, she, they saw	I, you, he, she, we, they seen
these	these ones
would have	would of
so am I	so aren't I
Come quickly!	Come quick!
different from	different than
be sure to	be sure and
can hardly	can't hardly

CHAPTER 7

Correcting Some Talk-Show Bloopers

Have some fun correcting these sentences overheard on our favorite talk shows:

1. Then her and my dad decided to get divorced.

2. Me and my sister were out on our own once.

3. Just because you got your freedom don't mean you can go out and do whatever you want.

4. Me and my girlfriend have been to Palm Springs.

5. I wouldn't let no boy touch me.

6. I'm not like that no more.

7. Knowing what I know now, I would of tried harder to make things work between he and I.

8. He was, like, you know, fun.

9. It don't really matter to me what he says.

10. As long as she's happy, so aren't I.

11. Everyone has to take responsibility for themselves.

12. I like have a lot of trouble with finances and stuff.

13. A woman drove up and she had South Carolina license plates on.

14. I have a long ways to go before I can even think about being in a relationship.

15. I try to get him to open up, but he just don't seem to have nothin' to say.

Answers: 1) she and my dad, 2) My sister and I, 3) you have, doesn't mean, 4) My girlfriend and I, 5) any boy, 6) anymore, 7) would have, between him and me, 8) He was fun, 9) It doesn't really matter, 10) so am I, 11) for himself or herself, 12) I have a lot of trouble with finances, 13) A woman who had South Carolina license plates on her car drove up, 14) a long way to go, 15) doesn't seem, anything to say.

A woman drove up and she had South Carolina license plates on.

CHAPTER 8

Some Common Mispronunciations

It's true that pronunciation often has a lot to do with the part of the country you're from. A Bostonian might say "*Aunt Florence*" like this: "*Awnt Florence*"; a Chicagoan, like this: "*Ant Florence.*" But some words are often mispronounced because the speakers don't know how to spell the word. On their mental blackboards, they see the word incorrectly and say it wrong. Here's our list of a few common mispronunciations. You may want to add a few of your own.

Say it like this:	Not like this:
across	acrost
affluent (aff-loo´-ent)	aff´-loo-ent
anticlimactic (anti-cli-mac-tic)	anti-cle-ma-tic
ask	ax
aspirin (as-per-in)	as-prin
chimney (chim-nee)	chim-lee
congratulate (con-grat-u-late)	con-grad-u-late
cooperate (co-op-er-ate)	cor-per-ate
coupon (cue-pon)	coo-pon
deteriorate (de-tere-i-or-ate)	de-tere-i-ate
environment (en-vi-run-ment)	en-vi-earn-ment

Say it like this:

Not like this:

Say it like this:	Not like this:
escape (es-scape)	ex-scape
experiment (ex-spare-i-ment)	ex-spear-i-ment
extraordinary (ex-stroar-din-ary)	extra-ordinary
fathom	phantom
forte (fort)	for-tay
frustrated	fustrated
genuine (gen-u-in)	gen-u-eyne
government (govern-ment)	gover-ment
height	heighth
huge (hyüj)	yooge
human (hyü-men)	yoo-men
jewelry (jool-ree)	joo-el-ree
library (lie-brar-ee)	lie-bare-ee
literal (lit-er-al)	li-tral
manufacture (man-u-fac-ture)	man-a-fac-ture
mischievous (mis´-che-vus)	mis-chee´-vi-ous
nuclear (new-klee-er)	new-cue-ler
pronunciation (pro-nun-cee-a-tion)	pro-noun-cee-a-tion
sandwich (sand-wich)	sam-widge or sam-which
stamina (sta-min-a)	stan-i-ma
supposedly (suppose-ed-ly)	suppose-eb-ly
them	'um
valedictorian (val-eh-dick-tor-i-an)	val-dick-tor-i-an
veteran (vet-er-an)	vet-trun